D0472830

MONARCH MAGIC!

Butterfly Activities & Nature Discoveries

WILLIAMSON PUBLISHING CO.

Library of Congress Cataloging-in-Publication Data

Rosenblatt, Lynn, 1945–
      Monarch magic!: butterfly activities & nature discoveries / photographs and text by Lynn M. Rosenblatt.
            p.   cm.
      "A Williamson good times! book."
      Includes index.
      Summary: Simple text and photographs depict the life cycle and metamorphosis of a monarch butterfly, from egg to caterpillar to chrysalis to emerging butterfly. Includes crafts and related activities.
      ISBN 1-885593-23-6 (alk. paper)
      1. Monarch butterfly—Juvenile literature.   2. Monarch butterfly—Study and teaching (Elementary)—Activity programs.
      [1. Monarch butterfly. 2. Butterflies.] I. Title.
      QL561.D3R668   1998
      595.78'9—dc21   98-34421
                                                         CIP
                                                         AC

Book design: **Joseph Lee Design, Inc.**
Illustrations: **Joseph Lee Design, Inc.**
Photographs: All photographs by **Lynn M. Rosenblatt**, with the following exceptions:
      Susan Hong (cover, bottom right; p. 20, top left; p. 47; p. 51, left)
      Rose McNulty (cover, bottom left; p. 6, right; p. 30, bottom; p. 66; p. 72, top; p. 74; p. 75; p. 77, top; back cover: top left and center)
      Glenn Moody (p. 29, bottom right; p. 70)
      Karen Oberhauser (p. 36)
      Monarch Watch (Ken Highfill p. 84; Janet Lanza p. 91, bottom right; O. R. Taylor p. 85 left, p. 91 bottom left; Jill Wells p. 63, bottom)
Printing: **Quebecor Printing, Inc.**

Printed in Canada

Williamson Publishing Company
P.O. Box 185
Charlotte, Vermont 05445
1-800-234-8791

10 9 8 7 6 5 4 3 2 1

A Williamson *Good Times!* Book

MONARCH MAGIC!

Butterfly Activities & Nature Discoveries

LYNN M. ROSENBLATT

WILLIAMSON PUBLISHING CO.

Acknowledgements

I eagerly share the success of this book with many caring and resourceful people: my devoted, loving, and supportive family; the staff at Williamson Publishing, with special thanks to Jack Williamson, Susan Williamson, and Emily Stetson; Joseph Lee, for his unique book design and creativity; Dr. Lincoln P. Brower, Distinguished Service Professor of Zoology Emeritus, University of Florida, for his extensive monarch research supported by the Wildlife Conservation Society; Donald A. Davis, The Friends of Presqu'ile Park, Brighton, Ontario; Elizabeth Donnelly, Journey North, Minneapolis, Minnesota; Orley "Chip" Taylor and Jim Lovett, Monarch Watch, University of Kansas, Lawrence, Kansas; Ro Vaccaro and Pat Herrgott, Friends of the Monarchs, Pacific Grove, California; Dr. Jane O'Donnell, Manager of Scientific Collections, University of Connecticut, Storrs, Connecticut; Bobby Gendron, Butterfly Encounters, Danville, California; Clayton Taylor, Connecticut Butterfly Atlas Project/Connecticut Butterfly Association; Dr. Karen Oberhauser, Monarch Butterfly Sanctuary Foundation, University of Minnesota; LuAnn Craighton, Callaway Gardens, Pine Mountain, Georgia; Mary Claffey, Science Center School, West Hartford, Connecticut; Kathy Read, monarch butterfly entrepreneur, Avon, Connecticut; Normand Surprenant, Brian Larson, and Robin Lawson, for their guidance and expertise in developing my photographs; Eileen Baukus, Ann Shea, and Carol Oriol-Jones, inspiring team-teaching colleagues; my friends, colleagues, and students at Andover Elementary School, Andover, Connecticut; my friends and creators of Connecticut's first butterfly house, The Living Courtyard at Webster Hill School, West Hartford, Connecticut; and Lee Larcheveque, creator of *The Butterfly King* video, whose devotion to raising and releasing monarch butterflies inspired my research and writing of *Monarch Magic!*

Dedication

This book is dedicated to protecting and preserving a natural phenomenon, the magical and magnificent monarch butterfly, whose habitat and destiny are at risk in our ever-changing world.

A donation is made to Friends of the Monarchs and the Monarch Butterfly Sanctuary Foundation for every book sold.

Contents

WILLIAMSON PUBLISHING CO.

The Monarch's Adventure

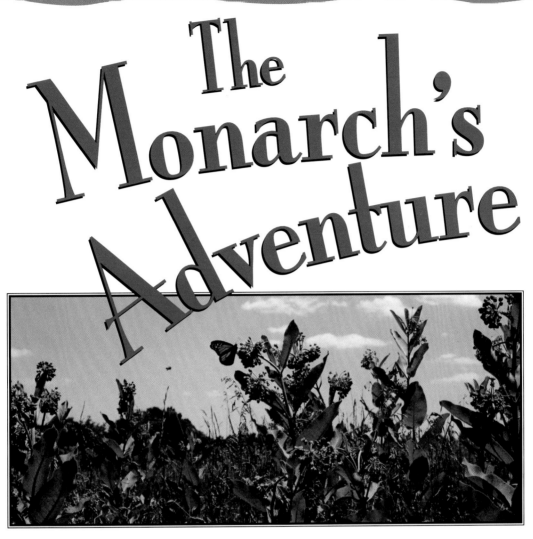

The monarch's amazing life story begins in a milkweed field.

Fluttering and gliding above the fragrant blossoms, the adult butterflies sip the milkweed flower's sweet nectar. Then, when the time is right, the female monarch begins laying hundreds of tiny, creamy white eggs on the underside of milkweed leaves, one egg per plant.

Let's Do It!

The Milkweed Connection

Turn to pages 42 and 84 to find out more about different types of milkweed in your area. You can help the monarchs by protecting milkweed and growing your own plants, so that the monarch butterflies will always have a home! See pages 60 and 88.

Track your discoveries in a butterfly journal as you begin your journey into the magical world of monarchs. See page 46.

Monarch mamas search very carefully for their special milkweed plants; in fact, milkweed is the only place a female monarch butterfly will lay her eggs! Monarchs belong in a family of butterflies called *milkweed butterflies*. They can't survive without the milkweed plant!

earching for monarch eggs is fun and easy. Just lift up a milkweed leaf and look underneath. You can tell monarch eggs by their dome shape and vertical lines that go up and down the sides of the egg, like a miniature cantaloupe or an igloo. Even hanging upside down, the eggs won't fall off the leaf, because the female butterfly uses a special "glue" to hold them in place. Though soft and yellow-white at first, the eggs will soon harden, turn gray, and darken as the black head of the baby caterpillar develops inside. If you find two or more eggs on one plant, or even on one leaf, it means several butterflies have chosen that place as an ideal butterfly nursery!

Eggshells for Breakfast

Inside the egg, a baby caterpillar is growing. In three to six days, a tiny, creamy white caterpillar — the size of the head of a pin, or about $1/16$ inch (1.5 mm) — chews its way out of the top of the shell.

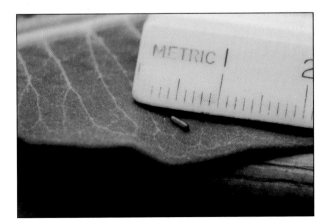

Next, it turns around and eats the broken shell. Yum!

It takes the caterpillar about six hours after its birth to develop its colorful black, yellow, and white stripes. Then, once properly dressed, the baby caterpillar begins its two most important jobs: eating milkweed leaves and growing.

You and Me, Kid

Do you eat eggshells for breakfast? Of course not ... you're a kid, not a caterpillar! But for baby caterpillars, the eggshell is a very important first meal, containing nutrients (food) necessary for the caterpillar's growth. Without it, the caterpillar might not develop properly. No skipping breakfast for you, baby caterpillar!

Getting to Know You, Caterpillar

Have you ever held a monarch caterpillar in your hand? Even the baby caterpillars are quite complex! Each monarch caterpillar has a head and 14 jointed parts called segments. *The head is easy to find. It has caterpillar chewing mouthparts and 12 small eyes, six per side. The eyes are called* ocelli *(oh-SEH-li). How silly!*

The first three segments behind the head form the thorax. *Each thorax segment has two jointed legs with sharp little claws on the end for gripping. (Eventually, these will become the six long, slender legs of the adult butterfly!) Attached to the thorax are two long, black tentacles. There's a shorter set at the caterpillar's back end, too.*

The rest of the segments form the caterpillar's abdomen. *Eight of these segments are easy to spot, but the last three are harder to see because they're fused, or joined, together. Five of the abdomen segments have a pair of "false" legs, or* prolegs, *a total of 10 in all. (They're called false legs because they aren't made like the caterpillar's true legs.) Each proleg has a tiny hook, or* crochet *(kro-SHAY), that helps it cling to things as it crawls.*

The caterpillar's "skin," or cuticle *(Q-teh-kul), is like a shell — it doesn't grow. And along the side of the caterpillar's body are holes, called* spiracles, *that let in air. What an unusual way to take a breath!*

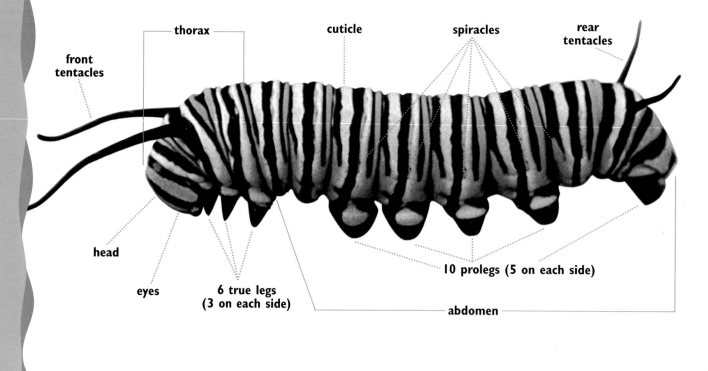

thorax

cuticle

spiracles

rear tentacles

front tentacles

head

eyes

6 true legs (3 on each side)

10 prolegs (5 on each side)

abdomen

The brightly colored monarch caterpillars (also called *larvae*) make their way to the top of the tall milkweed plants by climbing the thick, leafy stems. Once there, the caterpillars eat … and eat … and eat, munching on the most tender milkweed leaves. It's an easy menu to remember: milkweed for breakfast, milkweed for lunch, and milkweed for dinner!

Milkweed is a *host plant* to monarch butterflies because it is the only place that the female butterfly will lay her eggs and because it's the only food the caterpillars can eat. Each caterpillar gobbles up 20 to 30 milkweed leaves before it is full-grown. Monarchs must have milkweed.

munch …

munch …

munch …

Let's Do It!

Pom-Pom Caterpillar

Craft your own homemade caterpillar pet, complete with the head and segments, 12 small eyes, 16 legs, and 2 pairs of tentacles. See page 66.

As it eats, the caterpillar grows, and grows some more, until it finally grows too big for its colorful skin … so it sheds it!

A squeeze, a push, a tug, and a pull, and the butterfly-to-be lifts itself out of its tight old skin.

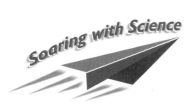

Do humans shed their skin? Not in the same way as a caterpillar. But your body grows fresh new cells every day and sheds the old cells. When you see flaky, dry skin turn white and peel off (such as after you've had a sunburn), you're shedding a layer of skin!

What other creatures besides caterpillars can you think of that outgrow their entire skin and shed, or molt? If you're thinking snakes, you're on the right track. Like the cuticle of the monarch caterpillar, a snakeskin won't grow as the snake gets bigger, so the snake sheds its skin instead!

Then, it rubs its face mask off ... turns around ...

and eats the shed coat. Delicious! This old skin, or cuticle, gives the caterpillar lots of vitamins and nourishment to grow big and healthy.

If you were to do as much eating and growing as a baby monarch caterpillar does during its first weeks of life, you'd weigh as much as a school bus just 15 to 20 days after you were born! That's some serious eating and growing!

The caterpillar eats and grows and sheds its skin not once ...

first shed
(³/16", ~4.5 mm)

not twice ...

second shed
(³/8", ~1 cm)

not even three times.

third shed
(³/4", ~2 cm)

Learning the Lingo

Each growing stage between sheds is called an *instar*.

It sheds four times before it is almost a full-grown caterpillar. And then it sheds once more!

fourth shed
(1 ¹/4", ~3 cm)

After each old skin is shed, a new outer skin hardens over the bigger body, and a new face mask forms over the caterpillar's larger head. By the time the caterpillar has shed four times and eaten enough to fill out its new skin, it measures 2 inches (5 cm) long — about the size of a Tootsie Roll®. But its weight is what is really surprising. It weighs almost 3,000 times more than it did when it was born!

full-grown caterpillar

A monarch butterfly sheds a total of five times in all — four times until it is almost full-grown, and then one final shed as it enters its next, mysterious, stage of life.

In My Monarch Journal

Hold a Caterpillar Weigh-in!

Watch nature at work! Chart a graph of a caterpillar's growth, following the directions on page 52. Jot down notes in your monarch journal about what the caterpillar eats each day, or make drawings of the changes that occur. You'll be amazed at how fast your crawling critter grows!

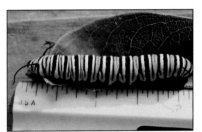

Let's Do It!

A Collector's Cater-Carton

Make a handy hiding place for all your small-sized treasures with a life-like or fanciful caterpillar! See page 70.

The Silk Button

After the caterpillar sheds its skin for the fourth time and eats enough milkweed leaves to grow into the new skin, it begins to wander.

Let's Do It!

Create a Cater-Poem

Want a caterpillar to crawl around a page in your monarch journal? See how on page 68.

By now, the roly-poly caterpillar has stored up enough energy for its next stage of life. A magical change is about to happen!

As it wanders, the caterpillar shows off its athletic skills. Like a miniature rock climber, it uses the *spinneret* just below its mouth to squeeze out a thin string of silky liquid to make a ladder of silk as it goes along.

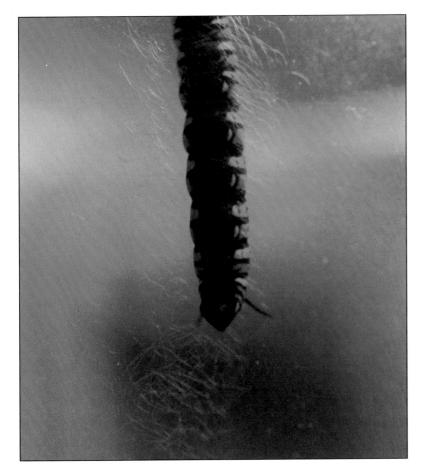

Squeeze ...

attach ...

crawl ...

squeeze ...

attach ...

crawl.

You and Me, Kid

Think of the spinneret as the caterpillar's built-in squirt gun. When you squeeze the trigger on a squirt gun, it shoots out a thin stream of water, similar to the way a monarch caterpillar squeezes out a stream of silk!

As soon as the caterpillar finds the perfect spot to rest, it begins to weave a lacy silk attachment to hang from. Each net of silk has a clump of white thread in the middle, called a silk "button."

Though it's called a "button," the caterpillar's silken spot is not really a button at all. Instead, it's a very secure place for the caterpillar to attach itself in the middle of its silk net (like a seat of Velcro®). The caterpillar may search for hours to find just the right branch or twig for building its special silk button. Once it's finished, the silk attachment is strong enough to withstand wind, rain, and storms!

To make the silken attachment, the caterpillar turns its head to the left, then to the right, back and forth … attaching silk here and there … piling up a neat lump of strong thread in the middle of the silk grid.

Once the silk button is made, the caterpillar turns its body around, and hangs from it!

How does the caterpillar hang on? It grips the silk with hooks located on the last set of prolegs (those funny, "false" legs). Then, when its rear end is firmly in place, it lets go of its hold, one proleg at a time.

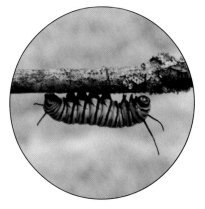

Let's Do It!

Raise and Release a Monarch

Watch the incredible transformation — from egg or caterpillar to chrysalis and butterfly — by raising a monarch yourself and releasing it into the wild. See page 47.

Slowly but surely, the caterpillar releases its grip, hanging lower and lower until it completely dangles upside down, like the letter J!

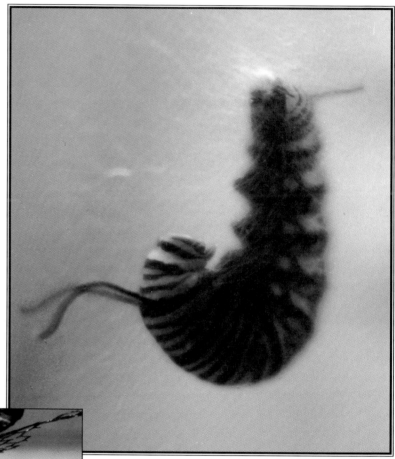

Securely attached to its silk button, the resting caterpillar gets ready for the magical change that will take place after its fifth, and final, shed — the amazing transformation from full-grown caterpillar to magnificent monarch butterfly. Farewell, caterpillar stage!

A Miracle of Nature

The Caterpillar Wiggle-Jiggle Dance

Antennae start a-quivering.
The body straightens out ...

Stripes begin to disappear
And skin is tossed about ...

Though this final skin-shedding feat may look easy, don't be fooled. This step takes some fancy footwork! Inside the skin at the rear end of the caterpillar's changing body lies the *cremaster*, a hornlike stalk with many hooks at the end. As the caterpillar wriggles out of its old skin, it inserts the cremaster securely into the silk button — without falling! It's a death-defying act!

Like all magic tricks, there's a secret. To avoid falling during this maneuver, the caterpillar holds onto its old skin (which is still attached to the silk button) with two hooks beneath the cremaster. Once secure, it lets go of the old skin.

It wiggles left.
It wiggles right.
It sheds off all its clothes ...

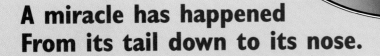

**A miracle has happened
From its tail down to its nose.**

**It changes to a chrysalis ...
Its body does not move.**

**Then little pearls begin to show
From deep within a groove.**

From its tail down to its nose, the caterpillar becomes a compact, smooth, oval-shaped, jade green *pupa*, the third stage of the monarch's life cycle. It has gone from egg to caterpillar, and now, with plenty of energy packed into its body, it prepares for its next, quiet stage of life. Pupa comes from the Latin word *pupa*, meaning "doll." And, like a doll, during its pupa stage in the *chrysalis* (which lasts about 14 days), the caterpillar looks life-like, but it doesn't move or eat at all!

The word *chrysalis*, describing the pupa's hard, clear outer shell, comes from the Greek word *chrysos*, which means gold. The color refers to the tiny specks, or "pearls" that appear on the outer shell of the chrysalis. Shimmering in the moonlight, the chrysalis — sheltering the green pupa inside — looks like a jewel of nature.

The outer skin turns crystal clear. The pearls turn into GOLD!

And deep within, two magic wings Are waiting to unfold.

Soaring with Science

Days 4-8

Can you think of another insect that eats only one kind of plant, spins silk, and forms a special resting place for its pupa stage? What about a silkworm? The caterpillar of the silkworm moth eats only mulberry leaves, and spins a silk cocoon, then pupates inside. The monarch caterpillar eats only milkweed leaves, spins a silk button, and forms a chrysalis under its skin as it molts for the final time.

Deep within the crystal sleeping bag of the chrysalis, amazing changes take place. During the two weeks in the chrysalis, the caterpillar's body-parts completely break down, change into a liquid, and are reformed into the organs and wings of a butterfly. It's magical, mysterious *metamorphosis*.

Days 9-11

Now, fully formed, the orange, white, and black butterfly is almost ready to burst into flight.

Days 12-14

You and Me, Kid

When you grow, your body gets bigger and bigger, yet you always have the same number of body parts: a head, a body, two legs and two arms, two hands and two feet. But it doesn't work that way for butterflies. Instead of the head, 14 segments, and 16 legs of a caterpillar, a butterfly has three distinct body parts and just six legs! And wings appear where there were no wings at all. The cells of the adult monarch butterfly that were lying *dormant*, or sleeping, within the body of the caterpillar awaken in the chrysalis stage and develop into adult butterfly parts! The butterfly stage is totally different than the caterpillar and pupa stages that came before. It's *metamorphosis*: a complete change.

The Special Day

Glistening and shining in the warm summer sun, the black, orange, and white-spotted wings of the monarch butterfly can be seen through the clear walls of the chrysalis. A butterfly is waiting to greet the day!

Early in the morning on its special day — four to six weeks since it first hatched from its egg — the monarch gets ready to make its break. It takes only a few seconds for it to emerge from its tight quarters. With a good push or two, the chrysalis door opens ...

A Closer Look

*A*fter the adult butterfly has formed, its body releases a liquid that loosens it from the chrysalis shell. Then its middle swells and pops the shell.

Just before emerging!

and the butterfly's head and part
of the body emerges.

Then, the full body emerges …

and by the third
push, the monarch is
free. Welcome to the
world, monarch!

Suspended upside down, the butterfly clings like a cliff-hanger to the outside of the chrysalis.

Warning! Danger!

Though we might think of basking in the sun as relaxing, the wet, newly emerged monarch butterfly faces one of the most dangerous times in its life! Butterflies are defenseless against predators such as birds during the hour or so it takes for their wings to dry out and their muscles to warm up.

The monarch's adult body is about $1^1/2$ inches (3.75 cm) long and the wings are wet and crinkled when they first emerge. But, in yet another surprise of nature, the butterfly pumps all the liquid from its fat abdomen into its wings. Watch closely: A reddish liquid may drip from its body. Don't disturb the butterfly during this important time! After 30 minutes or so, each wing reaches 2 inches (5 cm) in length.

Then, it's sun-bathing time, as the beautiful wings dry and harden for flight.

When the monarch is finally ready to fly, it spreads its wings wide open and then closes them tightly over its body, exercising and testing them.

Open wide ... close tight ... open wide ... close tight ... 1 ... 2 ... 1 ... 2 ... 1 ... 2 ... 1 ... 2.

That's the sign the butterfly is truly dry and ready for flight.

Let's Do It!

Paint a Monarch Magic T-Shirt

Now that you've seen the whole cycle from caterpillar to butterfly, stencil a T-shirt that shows them both off! See page 77.

antennae

head

compound eye

thorax

forewing

cells

wing vein

wing margins

hind wing

abdomen

Let's Do It!

Monarchs in Motion

Create a gliding butterfly mobile. See page 74.

A monarch butterfly's wings are designed to soar! Each of the monarch's wings is made up of two parts, a forewing and a hind wing. The outer rear edges of the wings, the *margins*, bend easily, pushing the air backward so the butterfly moves forward, while the thick, stiff front edges and base of the wings give the butterfly "lift." The butterfly's black veins form the framework of the wings, similar to the crossbars on a kite. With their lightweight bodies and large wings, monarchs are perfect long-distance gliders.

Life as a caterpillar is complete as the butterfly flies to a tasty flower to fuel up after weeks in the chrysalis without food. It spends the next few days eating and getting used to its body, smelling with its new antennae, tasting with its feet, and sipping nectar with its new straw-like *proboscis*. The monarch's leaf-munching days are over.

Learning the Lingo

Butterflies belong to the scientific category of insects called Lepidoptera, which means "scale wing." The words come from the Greek words *lepidos* (scale) and *pteron* (wing). If you look closely at each butterfly wing under a magnifying glass, you'll see thousands of tiny, flat scales that overlap like fish scales, or the shingles on a roof. These powdery scales give butterflies their beautiful colors and pattern shapes! To make your own pair of matching monarch wings, see page 54.

A Closer Look

The butterfly's proboscis, or tongue, is actually coiled up in the bottom of its face. When the monarch is ready to sip, it uncoils its proboscis and takes a drink of nectar. Yum!

Serve a Butterfly Feast

Give the butterflies in your neighborhood a buffet of sweetened fruit at your own butterfly cafe! Or, make your yard a butterfly retreat by planting a butterfly garden! See pages 82 and 83.

Butterfly, Butterfly, What Do You See?

... I see a rainbow looking at me! Did you know that butterflies have not one, not two, not even 100 eyes? Their compound eyes are made up of thousands of separate eyes. With so many eyes, butterflies can see more colors of the rainbow than any other insect in the world! Can you name the seven colors of the rainbow? (Hint: It spells ROY G. BIV!)

With its wings outstretched, the monarch butterfly soars in the sky and dances above the plants. It's no longer a baby egg or even a kid caterpillar anymore. Now it is all grown up, an adult butterfly. It glides and soars, looking for nectar and searching for a mate, so it can begin the cycle of life all over again.

Answer: red, orange, yellow, green, blue, indigo, violet.

female

male

A Closer Look

How do you tell the mama and papa monarchs apart? Look to the wings for the answer. Monarch males have two black dots, or scent glands, on their hind wings; female monarchs have no dots. It's as easy as that! Turn to page 75 to make your own mama and papa hand puppets.

But the monarch's tale isn't over yet. In fact, the butterfly's most amazing feat — a journey of thousands of miles — is just about to begin.

Summer's End

Most monarch butterflies live for just two to six weeks, soaring and gliding in the summer sunshine. They sip the nectar from milkweed and other flowers, mate, lay eggs on milkweed, and then die. From spring until fall, two to four generations of monarch butterflies hatch, live, mate, and die throughout the United States and in parts of southern Canada.

But the last generation of butterflies, the ones born in the late summer, are different. Unlike the butterflies that came before them, these monarchs don't mate, lay eggs, and die in a few short weeks. Instead, as the fragrant milkweed blossoms give way to majestic brown stalks crowned with pods of ripening seeds, these late-summer butterflies prepare for an incredible journey south, leaving the milkweed fields behind. As the first frost touches the milkweed fields and brisk autumn winds blow thousands of milkweed seeds into flight, the monarchs take flight as well.

POP!

POP!

POP!

Monarch Yearly Life Cycle

2nd to 4th Generations:
Several generations of monarchs may be born during the summer, depending upon the temperature and the length of each monarch's life. Adults mate and lay eggs.

1st Generation:
Adults mate and lay eggs.

New spring generation begins the cycle all over again.

Late-Summer Generation:
Adults fly south. They do not mate or lay eggs.

SUMMER

March April May June July August September October November December January February

SPRING

FALL

WINTER

Migrating monarchs mate, lay eggs, and die.

October through December
Late-summer monarchs arrive at wintering destinations.

With the warmer weather, these monarchs wake up, feed, and look for a mate.

Late summer monarchs overwinter in a semi-dormant state in winter, resting and conserving energy.

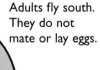

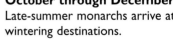

Monarchs can't live where temperatures are below freezing. To survive the winter, the late-summer monarchs *migrate*, or move, flying south to safe wintering sites in warmer areas. It's the miracle of the mighty monarch migration — the monarchs' incredible migratory waltz. Each year, hundreds of millions of monarchs from all over North America fly thousands of miles south to sites in California, Florida, and central Mexico — without a map!

Monarchs in Mexico's Oyamel fir trees.

This mysterious last generation of monarchs migrate as far as 2,500 miles south over a period of six weeks, to a spot they have never seen. Almost all of the monarchs east of the Rocky Mountains spend the winter resting in the ancient Oyamel fir trees in the cool, moist forests of central Mexico. They rest in trees at

With other creatures that migrate, such as birds and whales, the same individuals travel the route year after year to their winter and sum-mer grounds. But the monarchs that make the journey south have never been there before! They are totally on their own! Somehow, they know right where to go, arriving at the same sites in a thin strip of Mexican forest or to the same resting spots on the California coast where their ancestors have gone before them. Scientists don't know exactly how the butterflies do this, but they believe signals, such as the shortening daylight and colder temperatures, as well as the monarchs' own natural *instincts* (like an inner clock and compass) tell them when to go and where to fly.

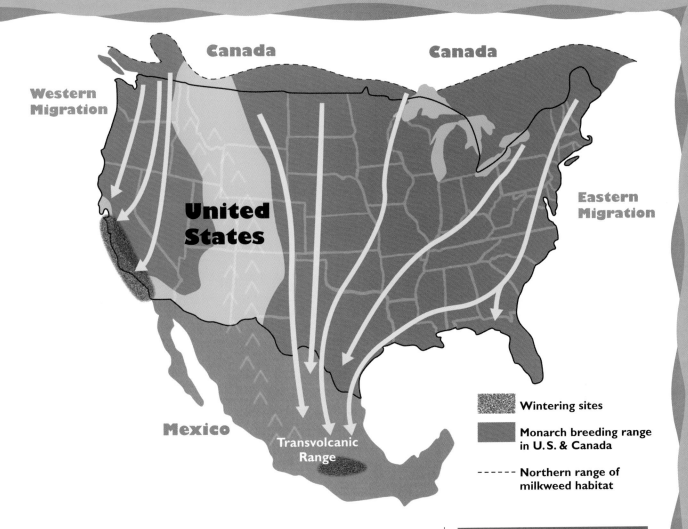

Canada   Canada

Western
Migration

United
States

Eastern
Migration

Mexico

Transvolcanic
Range

▦ Wintering sites

■ Monarch breeding range
in U.S. & Canada

----- Northern range of
milkweed habitat

an altitude of 9,000 to 11,000 feet (3,000 m) — nearly two miles up in the air! A few eastern monarchs fly down the Florida peninsula, and some even make it to the Yucatan Peninsula or Cuba.

Monarchs west of the Rockies migrate to sites in central and southern California, where the tired butterflies rest and quietly wait out the winter in the fog-covered pine and cypress groves and eucalyptus trees. Huddled close together for protection from wind, rain, and cold, the butterflies cover the trees in orange, white, and black.

Let's Do It!

Make a Fly-High Headband

Put on your wings and imagine that you are a mighty monarch flying south for the winter! Turn to page 72.

Be a Research Detective!

Visit the library or go on the Internet (see page 56) and hunt for information about the monarch butterfly or other living things that migrate. Use the key words butterfly, monarch, *and* migration *for your search. Then, come up with five facts about monarchs or migration that you never learned before, and write them down in your monarch journal.*

Let's Do It!

Watch Monarchs on the Go

Watch migrating monarchs where you live, or cooperate with other kids across North America on the Internet to follow the migration route of the monarch in the spring and fall. For more details, see page 58.

The next spring, as the warm sunshine awakens their bodies out of their *semi-dormant* (resting) state, the monarchs begin to fly again, and search for a mate. Then, they begin a return journey north. Most of the butterflies from Mexico will make it only as far as the Gulf States (Texas, Louisiana, Alabama, Mississippi, and Florida) before stopping to lay their eggs and die; in the West, where the distance is shorter, the monarchs may make it back to their original nesting grounds. The cycle then starts all over again … in a field of milkweed.

What's in a Name?

There are more than 90,000 different kinds of moths and butterflies in the world, but the monarch (scientific name Danaus plexippus) is one of the most beautiful and best-known. Even its common name tells how special it is: The word monarch means "ruler" or "king." In fact, it's thought that the monarch was named after England's King William, the Prince of Orange! Now that you know more about the monarch butterfly's amazing life cycle, would you consider it the king of the insect world? Write your ideas in your journal.

**Swallowtail
butterfly**

Make believe you are a migrating monarch butterfly. Your trip might begin as far north as Canada. Fluttering and soaring at altitudes as high as 10,000 feet (3,000 m) for six to eight hours a day, you would head toward your final destination in Mexico or California — a place you have never seen before! Some days you might travel as many as 100 miles (160 km).

Your trip might take six weeks ... almost as long as a summer vacation. What might you see along the way? Write a story about your journey in your monarch journal (see page 46). Give your tale a title and draw a picture to go with it.

Epilogue: Marvelous Milkweed

hink of all the times the milk-weed plant is mentioned in the story of the monarchs' amazing change from tiny caterpillar kids to beautiful butterflies. Is it mentioned six times? 10 times? Or is it mentioned more than 20 times?

The milkweed is mentioned so often because it is so very, very important to monarch butterflies. Without milkweed fields, there would be no monarchs at all.

Milkweed is as important to monarchs as fresh water is to people. No matter how much other food there is, people cannot survive without water. That's why we all work so hard to keep our water fresh and unpolluted. The same is true for milkweed and monarchs.

A Beautiful "Weed"

The magical milkweed, named for the milky white syrup that oozes from its leaves, is just like the seasons, putting on an amazing display throughout the year. The fragrant pink pom-poms in the spring, green pods in the summer, and the silky white seed puffs in the fall will razzle-dazzle you!

Even in the winter, milk-weed puts on a show, with its empty brown seed pods blanketed in snow.

Milkweed is certainly not just another weed that grows wild in the meadows. It is a natural wonder and — most important — it's the *host plant* for the magnificent monarch butterfly.

spring

summer

fall

winter

The Milkweed Milky Way!

Did you know that there are more than 100 species of milkweed growing across North America, from Canada to Mexico? Milkweed plants are members of the Asclepias (a-SKLEP-e-es) group of plants. The most familiar type in much of the eastern U.S. is common milkweed, with its big pink pompoms. In the Midwest, you might find swamp milkweed or prairie milkweed, and in the Southwest, sand milkweed or antelope horns milkweed might be more common. On the West Coast, a species called showy milkweed, with star-shaped pink and white flowers, is a favorite. Most states have several different milkweeds, and some — such as Oklahoma — are home to some 15 different types! For more about how to grow milkweed, see pages 83-91.

As a host plant, milkweed serves as the birthplace and then the food for monarch caterpillars, nourishing them so they can grow up to be beautiful monarch butterflies. High above the fields, female monarchs search for milkweed with eagle eyes. *Remember, mama monarchs will lay their eggs only on milkweed leaves.*

Then, once the caterpillars hatch from their eggs, milkweed is the only plant the baby caterpillars can eat! They don't eat tall grasses, or jagged oak leaves, or spiral leaves from lilies — just milkweed leaves.

Milkweed does more than just help baby caterpillars grow up into beautiful butterflies: It also protects monarchs by making them poisonous (and they taste terrible) to *predators* (hunters) like birds that might otherwise like a tender caterpillar or butterfly snack!

Milkweed and monarchs go together. But they need our help.

When we clear fields, build malls, and protect crops, we also kill monarchs and milkweed.

- Pesticides and insecticides used in farming to kill destructive insects and diseases also kill the monarchs or poison their drinking water.
- Herbicides, the chemicals sprayed on croplands to kill weeds, destroy wildflowers and milkweed.
- When open grassland or pasture is made into parking lots and shopping centers, milkweed fields are lost.
- Millions of monarchs get smashed by cars every year.
- In the mountains of Mexico, the monarchs' habitat is being destroyed by logging, while the pine and eucalyptus trees of coastal California are being lost to malls and houses and roads.

Somehow, we need to find a balance between keeping people happy and keeping the milkweed alive and the butterflies safe.

The good news is that it is not too late for each of us to make a difference in helping the monarchs, wherever we live.

Learning the Lingo

What's in the milkweed? Poisonous chemicals called *cardenolides* accumulate in the caterpillar's body and are passed on to the adult butterfly. The bright stripes on the caterpillar and butterfly are a warning flag to other critters, declaring, "Watch out! You'll get sick if you eat me!"

Kids Take Action!

You and your friends can make a big difference! Paint posters and banners for your school. Make bumper stickers for your family car. Design flyers and T-shirts with helpful sayings. See the activities on pages 60-64 for more ideas of what you can do to help the monarchs. Most important, get involved and

THINK MILKWEED!
SAVE THE MONARCHS!

In My Monarch Journal

Monarchs have been on the earth for more than 10 million years — more than twice as long as the first people. Yet, in the short time humans have been on this earth, we have had such a negative impact on the monarchs' habitat that monarchs, and their magical migration, are in danger of being lost forever. What do you think we can do to protect the monarchs and their habitat? Write your answer in your monarch journal.

Science Cycles and Environmental Explorations

Use what you know about the life cycle of the monarch (see pages 7-39) to join in on the action! Make your own butterfly journal to keep track of your discoveries, try your hand at copying nature's amazing symmetry, chart a caterpillar's growth as it eats and sheds, and help a monarch develop from egg to caterpillar to chrysalis to butterfly. Keep in step with the monarchs' migratory waltz — right from your own home! — by tracking the butterflies' journey to and from their winter resting grounds. And start an M & M Action Club to share your discoveries and to help save monarchs and milkweed!

Start a Monarch Journal!

A monarch journal is a great way to keep track of all your butterfly discoveries as you explore the magical world of monarchs and milkweed. Use it to design a butterfly garden, chart a caterpillar's growth, or record sightings of migrating monarchs. You'll find ideas throughout this book to guide you, but don't stop there! Take a photo of a monarch and tape it in your journal, or glue in a few milkweed seeds and flowers. Your monarch journal is your book of butterfly artwork and observations. *You* decide what goes in it. When you're done, you'll have a keepsake to look back on all year long.

WHAT YOU NEED:

- 2 sheets of construction paper (for the front and back covers)
- Art supplies (markers, watercolors, pencils, crayons)
- 20 to 30 sheets of white paper
- Scissors
- Stapler, or a paper punch and brass fasteners, ribbon, or twine

WHAT YOU DO:

1. Decorate one piece of construction paper for the front cover of your monarch journal. Draw your own milk-weed or butterfly design, or glue on photos or pictures of butterflies and milkweed. If you like, you can trace the butterfly on page 79 onto white paper, color it, and glue it to the front of your journal.
2. Give your monarch journal a title, such as [Your Name]'s Monarch Journal.
3. Place the sheets of white paper between the front and back covers. Staple the pages together along the left side, or punch three holes along the side and bind your journal with ribbon or brass fasteners.
4. Open your monarch journal to the first page, grab a pencil and some art supplies, and begin drawing, writing, graphing, and recording. Date each entry — even if it's just a brief note. The activities on the next pages will help get you started. Use your journal, and have fun!

Raise & Release a Monarch!

"I raised a monarch by myself!" ... and you can, too!

Experience the wonder of the monarch's life cycle and meta-morphosis, from egg to caterpillar to pupa (chrysalis) to butterfly, up close! You'll need a grown-up's permission before you start. Then, follow these easy steps, comparing the pictures of the life cycle here and on pages 7-33 with what you observe. Have fun, learn, and enjoy this truly amazing experience. It is one you will never forget!

WHAT YOU NEED:

- A cardboard box with a screen over top or a clear plastic (not metal) small animal cage with cover (such as a hamster cage)
- Fresh milkweed leaves (20 to 30 per growing caterpillar)
- Scissors
- Magnifying glass
- Grown-up helper

Butterfly Babysitting Basics

Raising a monarch butterfly from an egg or caterpillar takes dedication, patience, and love. It's a big responsibility! The little creature you are about to raise will depend entirely upon you for food and daily care, just as a pet tadpole, kitten, or gerbil would. Think of it as babysitting a butterfly until it is old enough to be on its own. It's up to you to keep it fed, healthy, and safe until it's ready to be released into its natural environment.

WHAT YOU DO:

The search

Take along your box or cage (never use a metal container, as it will get too hot). Explore a nearby meadow or field with a grown-up and look for milkweed leaves with holes. Try to find a black, yellow, and white striped monarch caterpillar crawling among the milkweed leaves.

Starting with an egg: If you find a monarch egg (look for the creamy white igloo-shaped eggs on the leaf's underside), break off the leaf and place it in your container. Wait for the egg to hatch. A tiny caterpillar should appear in three to six days.

Daily care

Place the cage outside under a chair or table away from direct sunlight. Or, put it inside where it gets sun and shade. A windowsill by an open window is perfect.

Clean your container every day and always keep it covered. (Lift the caterpillar, leaf and all, very gently when cleaning; it is very fragile and should not be handled.)

Give your caterpillar fresh milkweed leaves twice a day or as needed, and throw away old leaves. Baby caterpillars need tender leaves from the top of the plant. They'll consume 20 to 30 leaves each before they're grown! If a caterpillar is on an old leaf, don't pull it off. Instead, trim away the wilted leaf and leave the caterpillar in place. It will find its way to fresh food all by itself.

Starting with a caterpillar: If you find a caterpillar, don't pull it away from its leaf. Instead, break the leaf from the plant — caterpillar and all — and place it in your container. Then, cover the container, so the caterpillar can't escape.

Shedding

If your caterpillar remains still for several hours, don't disturb it! It may have woven a silk grid and be holding on as it gets ready to shed. Watch carefully, using your magnifying glass — a caterpillar sheds its skin quickly!

Collect the caterpillar's face masks that fall to the bottom of the container. Notice that with every shed the masks get bigger and bigger!

When your caterpillar is ready to shed for the fifth and final time, it will stop eating, travel to the lid of the container, weave a net grid, spin a silk "button," and then hang upside down for 12 to 15 hours.

Remove the lid. Ask a grown-up to hang the lid from a hook using the cage cover's handle, so you can watch what happens next. When the time is right, your caterpillar will begin to shed its skin for the last time. Watch as it wiggles out of its skin and changes into a beautiful chrysalis!

The butterfly

For the next 14 days, watch the chrysalis change from bright green to black and orange. The first week, the chrysalis will remain green. You'll see thin lines forming, and gradually the orange and black butterfly wings will become clearer. As the butterfly gets ready to emerge, it will pull away from the sides of the chrysalis. See pages 24-27 for the step-by-step photos.

Days 1-8: green chrysalis, wings begin to appear

Days 9-11: orange and black wings; green chrysalis

Days 12-14: wings and chrysalis become clearer

About an hour before emerging: The butterfly releases a murky liquid that helps free it from the walls of the chrysalis (see below).

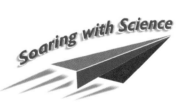

Have you ever watched polliwog eggs turn into tadpoles and become frogs? The way frogs grow is different from the way butterflies grow and different from how you grow. They're all examples of different life cycles — the changes that happen as living things grow and mature. Egg ... to caterpillar ... to pupa in its chrysalis ... and finally, to a butterfly. The monarch has four life cycle stages, each with a completely new look!

When the time is right, the chrysalis's sides will split open and a beautiful monarch butterfly will emerge! Watch closely so you won't miss the action — it will take only a few seconds.

Wait 1 to 2 hours. Then, gently place your finger or a stick under the butterfly's body and let it crawl on its own and grab hold.

Bring your butterfly outside and place it on a flowering plant or bush to rest and dry its wings for the next few hours. When the butterfly is ready, it will fly away.

Let's Do It!

Take a Metamorphosis Hunt!

Where can you look for evidence that this magical metamorphosis has taken place in nature? You know the signs: chewed leaves, discarded skins, face masks, an empty chrysalis. What other clues has nature left behind that tell you of changes? Think of bird egg shells, wasps' papery nests, fossils, and decaying trees. Nature is ever-changing, and you can watch her show, any time and any place!

For the Record

Caterpillars do lots of eating and growing, shedding their skin as it becomes too tight! Chart, or graph, a caterpillar's growth in your monarch journal to get an idea of just how fast caterpillars grow, and keep a record of when and how much your caterpillar eats. The results may surprise you!

Graph It!

A graph is a factual picture that allows you to see nature at work. It helps you to see facts that are sometimes very hard to imagine — like the growth spurt of a baby caterpillar (see pages 9-15). Picture yourself (or your brother or sister) weighing 12 tons, or as much as a school bus, just two weeks after being born, and you'll get the idea. Pretty hard to imagine, right? But a graph is something like that picture — it shows how something changed and how much time it took to change, too.

WHAT YOU NEED:

- Graph paper
- Pencil
- Tape measure or ruler
- Monarch egg or caterpillar (see Raise and Release a Monarch!, page 47)
- Monarch journal (see page 46)

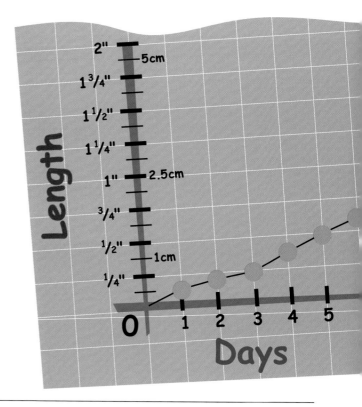

A Life History Log

Keeping a day-by-day written record about your caterpillar's changes is another way to preserve an image of what happens. You may want to jot down notes in your monarch journal about how many leaves your caterpillar eats each day or make drawings of what occurs as the caterpillar grows and changes into a chrysalis and a butterfly. Or, take a photograph each day to glue in your journal, and write down what you observe.

WHAT YOU DO:

1. To make a growth graph, write the dates, starting with the day the caterpillar emerges, across the bottom of a piece of graph paper. Along the left side of the page, write lengths in ¹/8" (3 mm) progressions going up the page to 2" (5 cm).

2. At the same time each day (say, every morning at 9:00), measure the caterpillar, using the ruler or tape measure. Lay the ruler next to the caterpillar on the leaf. You won't need to actually touch the caterpillar.

3. On the graph, put a dot at the appropriate measure mark every day, even if the caterpillar doesn't grow.

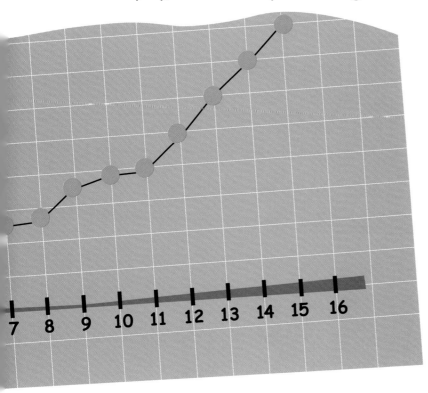

4. Connect the dots with a line, and tape the graph in your monarch journal.

5. What can you tell from your graph? Did your caterpillar grow about the same amount every day, or did it grow in spurts? What day did it grow the most? the least? Were there any days when it didn't grow at all? Remember, caterpillars stop eating just before they shed.

6. Write down what you observed. Draw a picture (with the date) to go with your chart.

Tell a True (or Tall) Caterpillar Tale!

There once was a…Pretend you're a tiny baby caterpillar just beginning your life on a giant milkweed plant. Write a story in your monarch journal, or take turns creating a story with one other person, or with a whole roomful of people. Before you begin, decide whether your story is going to be based on facts (as in this book) or fantasy (maybe your pretend caterpillar sips milkshakes!). See where your story takes you. Here's a line to get you started: "The wind was howling and the thunder roared on Planet Milkweed the day I was born…."
Now you take a turn!

Wing Symmetry:

Think back to when the butterfly emerged from its chrysalis (see page 26). Within a short time, the butterfly spread its beautiful, *symmetrical* (matching) wings — four wings, two on each side. With the monarch in mind, here are some ways to explore symmetry in nature.

Symmetrical Glob Art

Fold a piece of 8 1/2" x 11" (21 cm x 27.5 cm) paper in half. Open it up so it lays flat. On one side only, place globs of different-colored paint in a butterfly wing shape; then, refold it closed. Press it lightly.

Unfold the paper so it lays flat. What do you notice? That's right, you've made an exact print of the blob design on both sides of the paper — the same way butterfly wings work in nature. It's symmetry!

Create Wing Patterns

Here's a fun — and tasty — game to play with a partner. Take turns going first. Trace the outer shape of the butterfly on page 79 or draw one freehand. Use M&M®s, dried beans, cereal, macaroni shapes, jelly beans, raisins, nuts, and other small edible items to make your creation. First, you place a piece; then, your friend places a piece to match your side, continuing until the wings are full and symmetrical. (For best results, place pieces very close together.)

Nature's Look-Alikes

Monarch Mirrors

Here's a fun way to discover the symmetry in a butterfly's wings, but you'll need to look carefully, practicing your "observing" role as a scientist! Place a piece of white paper over this shaded-out right wing in the monarch photo. Then, looking very carefully, draw the right wing on the paper, copying exactly what you see on the left wing. Color it the same colors, too. Now, leave your drawing for a while and come back to it later. Compare the right and left wings. How'd you do?

Nature's Symmetry

Many living things — insects, animals, even humans — have a natural symmetry.

• Take a look in the mirror and see for yourself. What features do each side of your body share? What smaller characteristics are different? Put them together and you have wonderful you!

• Go on a symmetry search. Outdoors, see how many different things you can find in nature that are symmetrical. Look at the shapes of trees, shells, animals, and flowers for starters. Make a leaf rubbing: Placing several separate leaves under white paper, and rub a crayon across the top of the paper, highlighting the veins of the leaves. Is the leaf symmetrical or not?

You can find symmetry indoors, too. Start with the shape of this book; then, do a symmetry search throughout your house. How have humans given balance to their world by copying nature?

The Mighty Monarch Migration

Chart the monarchs' amazing migration (see pages 34-39) across North America! For a first-hand view of the migration, visit a monarch viewing site in your area, or join with other kids across the continent to map the migration path on the Internet ... and find out how you can help save the monarchs' winter resting grounds!

Monarchs on (and off) the Web

Journey North

This program on the Internet lets you follow the migration route of monarchs and other migratory animals to and from Mexico. Kids cooperating with other kids make this great program work. For instance, kids in Texas see the butterflies and notify kids in Alabama. Alabama kids notify Mississippi, and so on, all the way up the coast and back again in the fall. Trace the map on page 59 and write in the dates that the monarchs pass through different states, including your own!

Journey North, 125 North First St., Minneapolis, MN 55401; (612) 339-6959.
E-mail: jnorth@jriver.com
Website: http://www.learner.org/jnorth/

Monarch Monitoring Project

Based at the Cape May Bird Observatory in Cape May, New Jersey, this group monitors migrant monarch populations along the East Coast.

MMP, c/o Dick Walton, CMBO, 600 Route 47 North, Cape May Courthouse, Cape May, NJ 08210.
Website: http://www.concord.org/~dick/mon.html

Friends of the Monarchs

This nonprofit community organization tracks migration sightings and is dedicated to preserving and restoring the monarch butterfly habitat in Pacific Grove, California.

Friends of the Monarchs, P.O. Box 51683, Pacific Grove, CA 93950; information at 1-888-PG MONARCH and (408) 375-0982, or Butterfly Town USA tourist information.
Website: http://www.pacificgrove.com/butterflies

Monarch Watch

This group of students, researchers, teachers, and volunteers throughout the U.S. and Canada monitors the flight patterns of monarchs to and from Mexico. The Web site has a wealth of information on monarchs, migration, and milkweed.

c/o Orley "Chip" Taylor, Dept. of Entomology,
Univ. of Kansas, Lawrence, KS 66045; 1-888-TAGGING
or 1-913-864-4441 for viewing information.
E-mail: monarch@ukans.edu
Website: http://www.monarchwatch.org/

The Monarch Program/California Monarch Sites

This group monitors migrations, preserves overwintering habitats, and supports educational programs and conservation through butterfly gardening.

Dr. David Marriott
Monarch Program, P.O. Box 178671,
San Diego, CA 92177; (760) 944-7113, or 1-800-606-6627.
E-mail: Monarchprg@aol.com

The Western Monarch Migration Project

The Pacific Northwest portion of the Monarch Rescue Project monitors monarch butterflies and milkweed populations.

Dr. Dan Hilburn, Oregon Dept. of Agriculture,
635 Capitol St. NE, Salem, OR 97310-0110; (503) 986-4663.
E-mail: dhilburn@oda.state.or.us

Midwest Monarch Project

Kids can study the beauty and mystery of the monarch butterfly.

MMP, 3116 Harbor Dr. SE, Rochester, MN 55904.
E-mail: 0535qhno@informns.k12.mn.us

Help Save the Monarchs' Resting Grounds!

The fog-covered fir trees in the central Mexican highlands and the Monterey pine and eucalyptus trees of Pacific Grove provide a perfect climate, a microclimate, with just the right moist air, light, shade, temperature, and wind protection for the monarchs to live over the winter. Resting in temperatures just above freezing, the monarchs wait out the winter in a sleeplike state, conserving their energy for the long journey home.

Sadly, these ideal wintering grounds are in danger. Logging of the ancient fir forests in Mexico's Transvolcanic Range is destroying the eastern monarchs' winter sanctuaries, and in the West, monarchs are being squeezed out of their wintering sites by dwindling open space and constant coastal development. It's as if the butterflies' winter coats are being torn away!

What can you do to help? Write letters to get people to preserve the monarchs' sanctuaries, and plant milkweed and other plants for the butterflies. Or write to the **Monarch Butterfly Sanctuary Foundation** (c/o Dr. Karen Oberhauser, 2078 Skillman Ave., Roseville, MN 55113), dedicated to protecting and preserving the monarchs' overwintering habitat in Mexico. See pages 60-64 to find out more about how you can help the monarchs.

Visit a Monarch Look-Out

Monarchs can be seen throughout most of the United States and in southern parts of Canada. Depending on where you live, you can watch them as they migrate to Mexico and back, or on their journey to and from sites along the California coast.

There are numerous "look-outs," known as favorite resting places for traveling monarchs. Look on the map for just a few of the many spots that are famous butterfly stopping points. There are many more sites than are listed here. Take a day trip to one of these resting places or travel for a weekend of adventure during the fall and again in the spring for the return migration. The journey begins in late August at the northernmost sites, reaching the destinations in October and November, or even early December. Don't forget to bring binoculars: During peak migrations, it's possible to see thousands of butterflies passing through at once! For a more complete list of sites near you and best times for viewing, contact one of the organizations listed on pages 56 and 57.

West Coast

Late August through November
1. British Columbia, Canada
2. Deshutes River Recreation Area, Deshutes State Park (near Rufus, OR)
3. Lava Bed National Monument (near Tulelake, CA)
4. Ventura, CA
5. San Francisco (East Bay)
6/7. Natural Bridges State Beach & Lighthouse Field State Park, Santa Cruz, CA
8. Pacific Grove, CA (also known as Butterfly Town, USA), where many monarchs west of the Rocky Mountains spend the winter.
9. Monterey, CA
10. Morro Bay, CA
11. Pismo Beach, CA

Midwest & Central

Late August to early October
12. Duluth, MN
13. Minneapolis, MN
14. Glencoe, MN
15. Des Moines, IA
16. Malvern, IA
17. Midland, MI
18. Shawnee, KS
19. Ardmore, OK
20. Ector, TX
21. Fort Worth, TX
22. Bronte, TX
23. Midland, TX
24. Pecos County, TX
25. Brenham, TX
Note: There are many more sites than are listed.

Butterfly Houses, Sanctuaries, Gardens, Conservatories

Visit these special butterfly centers to get a first-hand look at monarchs throughout the year.

A. Butterfly Pavilion and Insect Center, Westminster, CO (open year-round)
B. The Butterfly Place at Papillon Park, Westford, MA (open mid-April through mid-October)
C. Butterfly World, Coconut Creek, FL (open year-round)
D. Marine World Africa USA's Butterfly World, Vallejo, CA (open year-round)
E. Day Butterfly Center at Callaway Gardens, Pine Mountain, GA (open year-round)
F. Cockrell Butterfly Center, Houston Museum of Natural Science, Houston, TX (open year-round)
G. Niagara Parks Butterfly Conservatory, Niagara Falls, ON, Canada (open year-round)

East Coast

Late August
26. Trenton, ON, Canada
27. Burlington, ON, Canada

Early to mid-September
28. Point Pelee National Park, ON, Canada (near Windsor)
29. Maumee Bay State Park, Toledo, OH

30. Watch Hill, RI
31. Hammonassett Beach State Park, Madison, CT
32. Cape May Point Bird Observatory, Cape May, NJ
33. Point Lookout, MD (in St. Mary's County)
34. Chincoteague National Wildlife Refuge, VA (eastern shore of Chesapeake Bay)

Late September to October
35. Pensacola, FL
36. St. Mark's National Wildlife Refuge, St. Marks, FL (Annual Butterfly Festival the 3rd week of October)
37. Miami, FL

Canada

Canada

United States

Mexico

Mexico
Early October through November
38. Monclova
39. Saltillo
40. San Luis Potosi
41. Zacateca
42. Queretaro
43. Angangueo
44. El Campanario

Transvolcanic Mountain Range

Form an M&M Action Club!

(Monarchs and Milkweed)

Now that you know about monarchs and milkweed (and the monarchs' migration), it's time to take some action! Form an M & M club with friends, classmates, and neighbors. Welcome everyone — young and old — who wants to share in some monarch fun. Serve orange and black (brown) M&M®s in honor of Monarchs & Milkweed, or Migrating Monarchs. While you are munching, plan picnics, outings, a trip to a monarch viewing site, and Save the Monarch activities.

Get the Word Out!

You know how important the milkweed fields and the winter resting sites are to the monarchs. Now let other people know! You'll be surprised at how many people will get involved to save the monarchs — but first they need to know what's happening to the monarchs' habitat. Here's what you can do to help:

Have a contest to write the best slogan for saving the monarchs and the milkweed fields. Invite everyone in your neighborhood or school to enter.

Paint posters and banners for your school, town hall, and community library. Make bumper stickers for your family car. Design flyers and T-shirts with helpful sayings. (See page 77 for details.)

Ask a teacher if your class could work on a community project, such as growing a school milkweed or butterfly garden, to increase people's awareness about the monarch and the disappearing milkweed fields and monarch winter resting grounds.

Monarchs & Milkweed Club

Come to our meeting: Earn a "Wing" badge.

Make new friends

Have fun!

Collect seeds!

Raise & release!

Plant milkweed!

Declare Monarch Awareness Week. Monarchs can have their own local — or national — day! Put up flyers around town and invite everyone to your next M & M Club meeting. Organize a trip to a monarch observation site or sanctuary near you (see page 58), and invite the public to come along. Or find a monarch site on the Internet (see page 56), and get kids across the country to join in on the action, counting and celebrating monarchs in their area.

Write letters to the editor of your local newspaper, your state's environmental protection agency, and the people in your city and state government, telling about the plight of monarchs and milkweed. Ask them to support laws that save open lands and help preserve wildlife habitats. Kids' letters *do* make a difference!

Save the Monarchs' Playground!

Stand quietly with your friends in a milkweed field. Watch the butterflies. Smell the sweet fragrance of the field. Listen to the sounds. Bring your camera and take turns photographing what you see.

Now, imagine what it would be like if this field became a parking lot or a mall. Then, discuss with your friends what you can do to save the monarchs' habitat. Here are some ideas to get you started.

Host a "Transplant a Milkweed" day: Hayfields and meadows are often mowed for hay or plowed by bulldozers for parking lots and malls ...

and so is the milkweed! If we all worked toward transplanting milkweed to new areas that aren't needed for development, think how much milkweed we could save! (Turn to page 88 for tips on transplanting milkweed.)

Plant nectar sources for butterflies by growing a butterfly garden, including milkweed, of course, as one of the plants (see page 83).

Collect and distribute milkweed seeds. Learn how to save the seeds for fall or spring planting so you can begin a new milkweed garden in a backyard, school yard, or park. Pass them out in sandwich bags, with planting instructions tucked inside, so your neighbors and friends can grow some, too. Even a patio pot can be a milkweed garden spot. (See page 90 for more on how to collect milkweed seeds.)

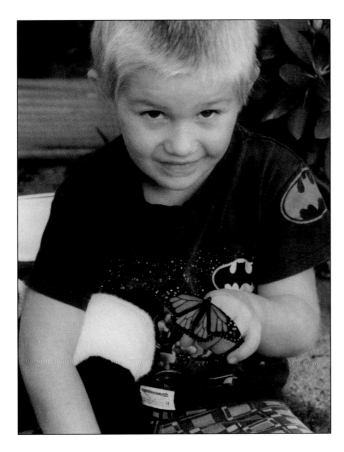

Teach a friend to raise and release. Butterflies sip nectar from milkweed blossoms in or near orchards and vegetable fields that may be sprayed with pesticides. You and your friends can rescue the eggs and the caterpillars, and then raise and release them as butterflies! (See page 47.)

Keep butterflies safe. Butterflies are flying over busy streets and highways every day. Cars and trucks are everywhere. By planting milkweed fields and gardens in safe places away from traffic, we help the butterflies stay safe.

Organize a fund-raiser!

One way to get involved is to raise some money for your club activities, so that you can do even more to help the monarchs. Use the money to buy seeds for milkweed or butterfly gardens, or to fund a school or home website about monarchs or milkweed. Contribute some of your funds to a Save the Monarch foundation. Here are some ideas of what you can do:

Have a bake sale. Decorate cupcakes and cookies in orange and black. Ask a local store for permission to set up a table outdoors on a weekend.

Sell T-shirts, butterfly headbands, mobiles, and puppets that you make at a club meeting. (See pages 72-79.)

Hold a bottle drive. Offer to pick up bottles in your local neighborhood, as well as in parks. It's a good way to clean up your town and raise money.

Caterpillar Capers

What's black and white and yellow all over? A monarch caterpillar! Put your caterpillar know-how (see page 10) to use and have some fun. Craft an almost life-like caterpillar pom-pom pet, write a silly (or serious) cater-poem, and paint a fanciful collector's cater-carton. The directions on pages 66-70 will get your started. Then, take off on caterpillar capers of your own!

Pom-Pom Caterpillar

Here's a wiggly monarch caterpillar — proportioned like a real one — that you can keep as a special "pet." Put it on a shelf, your bed, or with your stuffed animal collection.

WHAT YOU NEED:

- Body: (12) 1" (2.5 cm) black pom-poms
- Head: 2" (5 cm) black pom-pom or Styrofoam® ball
- Legs and tentacles: Black pipe cleaners
- Eyes: (12) ¼"-diameter (5 mm) plastic eyes
- Yellow and white tempera paint
- Scissors, glue, paper towels, paper plates

WHAT YOU DO:

To make the body

1. Dip the sides of one black pom-pom first into the yellow paint and then into white paint.
2. Working on a paper towel, place the painted pom-pom next to the head, and press hard! (The paint acts like glue.)
3. Dip and stick all the other pom-poms together, side by side. Let them stick to the paper towel. You'll have a head and 12 segments — 3 for the thorax and 9 for the abdomen, with the last pom-pom representing the 3 fused segments.
4. Allow your caterpillar to dry overnight. The next day, cut away the paper towel, but leave some paper underneath for support.

top view

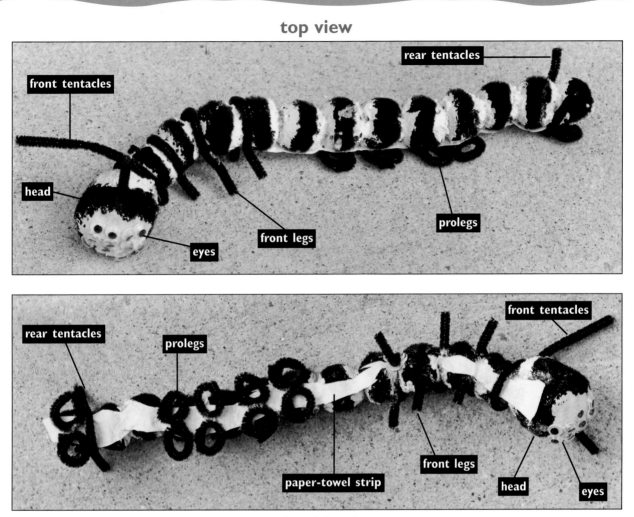

top view

front tentacles

rear tentacles

head

eyes

front legs

prolegs

rear tentacles

prolegs

front tentacles

paper-towel strip

front legs

head

eyes

underside view

To complete your caterpillar

Front tentacles: Cut an 8" (20 cm) length of black pipe cleaner and wrap it between head and first segment.

Rear tentacles: Cut a 4" (10 cm) length of pipe cleaner and wrap it around the last segment.

Front legs: Cut three 4" (10 cm) lengths of pipe cleaner. Bend each into a U and hook them over the first three body segments, starting behind the head.

10 prolegs: Cut pipe cleaners into ten 2" (5 cm) lengths, and form them into circles. Turn the caterpillar over.

Counting from the head:
- Glue 2 proleg circles side by side, so they stick out on opposite sides of segments 6, 7, 8, and 9. Skip 10 and 11. (You should have used eight pipe cleaner circles.)
- Glue the last two circles on the last segment (representing the fused segments).

Eyes: Glue all 12 eyes onto the head, 6 eyes on each side.

Pick up a milkweed leaf from the ground so your "caterpillar" can munch away while resting on your desk or bookcase.

Create a Cater-Poem!

Creating pictures with words is as much fun as creating caterpillar and butterfly crafts — and all you need is paper and pencil! To get started, think of words that create an image or picture in your mind, describing butterflies, caterpillars, or milkweed, and write them in your monarch journal.

14 segments, a head,
And 12 small eyes

A yellow, black,
And white surprise.

Two black tentacles,
Front and back

Guard against
A bird attack.

Brightly colored,
Prey will stare

Hungry birds
Beware, beware!

Delightful Diamonds

Building a diamond with words, you say? Sure, and it is easy, too. And don't forget, poetry can be silly or serious, accurate or fanciful. After all, it is *your* poem!

WHAT YOU DO:

1. Choose two different subjects — like caterpillars and milkweed. In pencil, lightly number seven lines on your paper.
2. Write down the first subject (a noun) on Line 1, and the other subject on Line 7.
3. Write two words that describe each subject (adjectives) on Lines 2 and 6, centering the words to make the diamond shape.
4. Write three action words (verbs) on Lines 3 and 5.
5. On Line 4, write two nouns similar to the first subject, followed by two words similar to the second subject. You can use a slash mark to divide the groups of words. Erase the numbers and look at your diamond!

CATERPILLAR

BRIGHT   BUMPY

CRAWLING   MUNCHING   SHEDDING

CHRYSALIS   MONARCH / SEEDS   NECTAR

GROWING   FLOWERING   BURSTING

PINK   WHITE

MILKWEED

black = subject
purple = adjectives
green = verbs
orange = nouns

Munching milkweed
Is a plus

Milkweed makes them
Poisonous!

16 legs to crawl and play
10 will vanish, 6 will stay

Spinning silk,
Now that's a fact

Upside down
They do an act!

Wiggle, jiggle, watch –
don't miss!
They change into a
chrysalis!

Caterpillar, not a
trace ...
Fluttering wings now
take its place!

This diamond-shaped poem is called a *diamante* (dee-ah-MAHN-tay) poem. Diamante is a French word meaning diamond. The words shape the pattern in seven lines.

Colorful & Concrete

Concrete poems give you two ways to create a picture — a shape and descriptive words! That's because a concrete poem is written in the shape of its subject. Create your poem in the shape of a wiggly caterpillar or a butterfly with outstretched wings. You can use single words or phrases on any lines to give your poem — and your butterfly or caterpillar — its shape.

magical monarch   magical monarch
fluttering   fluttering
chrysalis   chrysalis
munch   munch
pretty   pretty
egg   egg
pretty   pretty
munch   munch
chrysalis   chrysalis
fluttering   fluttering
migrating south   migrating south

Get the idea? Take off on your own!

Collector's Cater-Carton

Here are 12 caterpillar compartments to store all your small-sized treasures in! You know exactly how a live monarch caterpillar looks (see page 10). Here, you can make your cater-carton as "real" or fanciful as you like.

WHAT YOU NEED:

- Cardboard egg carton (1-dozen size)
- Tempera paint (in black, yellow, and black, or colors of your choosing)
- Tape or stapler
- Black pipe cleaners
- Scissors

WHAT YOU DO:

Face: Cut off the top of the egg carton. Using a mug or glass, trace a circle on it and cut out.

Tentacles: Bend a 6" (15 cm) piece of pipe cleaner into a V. Staple it to the head and the end.

Legs: Cut pipe cleaners into 6" (15 cm) lengths. Bend each one into a U and hook over the body between egg cup segments. Bend up the ends of the pipe cleaners to make feet. Follow leg placement pattern on page 67, or make as many legs as you wish.

Body: Cut the egg carton bottom in half lengthwise. Tape both halves together, end to end, so you have 12 body segments (the last cup can represent the fused segments on a real caterpillar). With the open side of egg cups up, tape or staple the circle face to one end of the body. Paint the face and body if you wish, and let it dry.

Use your cater-carton often, and make another one for a friend!

Monarch Fun

Imagine yourself as a monarch, fluttering above milk-weed plants, sipping nectar from flowers, and soaring south on your journey to the mountains of Mexico or to the forests of the Pacific coast. Or, perhaps you've just emerged from the magical chrysalis and are trying your wings on their first flight. Bring your imaginings to life with a fly-high headband, monarch mobile, and flutter-by puppet. Stencil and paint a monarch T-shirt to wear and butterfly stickers to decorate your journal and notebooks. The activities on the following pages are sure to make your spirits soar, wherever your flights of fancy take you.

Fly-High Headband

Put on your wings and pretend you are a mighty monarch, migrating south for the winter! Your strong wings will take you thousands of miles across North America ... over the rivers ... over the mountains ... and over the fields of milkweed. How does it feel to be a butterfly? What do you see as you glide and soar? Fly high, little butterfly, fly high!

WHAT YOU NEED:

- Construction paper, black or white
- Scissors and tape
- 1 sheet white paper, 8½" x 11" (21 cm x 27.5 cm)
- Butterfly stencil (see page 79)
- Black, yellow, and orange crayons or markers
- 12" (30 cm) black pipe cleaner

WHAT YOU DO:

To make the headband: Cut two strips of construction paper, each about 1" x 12" (2.5 cm x 30 cm). Tape them together end to end.

To make the wings: Trace the monarch stencil (see page 79) onto the white paper and color it. Fold your drawing in half and cut along the fold line. Carefully cut around each half. Cut off the stencil antennae.

To make antennae: Fold the pipe cleaner in half and shape it into a V. Tape it to the middle of your headband. Bend up the tips for knobs.

To attach butterfly: Lay your butterfly halves in place, colored side up and facing each other. Remember, a monarch's wings are *symmetrical*, or matching, so you'll need to line them up carefully! Tape the wings and antennae to the headband.

Ready, set, fly: Fold the wings over the headband strip so they point outward. Ask a grown-up to fit the headband to your head and tape the ends together.

Now try your wings!

Monarchs-in-Motion Mobile

Create your own flock of monarchs to glide in the wind on a warm, sunny day.

WHAT YOU NEED:

- Small branches or twigs
- Green pipe cleaners
- Green yarn
- White paper
- Crayons or markers
- Scissors
- Thread or fishline

WHAT YOU DO:

1. Break the branches or twigs into two 12"-long (30 cm) sections, four 8"-long (20 cm) pieces, and four 6" (15 cm) pieces. Criss-cross each pair of same-size twigs, forming an X or star shape (you'll have five pairs in all). Tie each set of twigs together with a green pipe cleaner.
2. Assemble the base of the mobile by hanging one of the four smaller twig Xs from each of the four larger branch ends, using green yarn.
3. Draw 16 to 18 butterflies on paper. Color; then, cut them out. Attach a piece of thread or fishline to each butterfly's head or body.
4. Hang a butterfly from each of the 16 twig ends. Any extra butterflies can hang from the main branches.

5. Add a pipe cleaner loop to the top of your mobile to hang it up. Then open a window and let the breezes blow!

Fly, Monarchs, Fly!

With their big wings and light-weight bodies, monarchs are excellent gliders. By flapping their wings slowly, they can fly thousands of miles! (Turn back to page 30 to get the science behind this mystery of flight.)

Hung Up?: If twigs and branches aren't available, use two coat hangers, arranged in an X and fastened together at the top with tape or pipe cleaners, as the base for your butterfly mobile.

Add a "Grape" Chrysalis!

Separate one or two green grapes from a bunch, leaving the tiny stem on the grape. Use thread to tie each grape to a branch of your mobile. Paint tiny gold dots on each grape to represent the "golden pearls" on the outside.

Flutter-By Hand Puppet

Imagine what fun a monarch butterfly must have flying over the flowers, dancing among the blossoms, sipping sweet nectar, and playing in the warm summer sunshine. Take your puppet outdoors and have it soar over the marigolds and glide over the zinnias to get a sense of a monarch's beautiful world. Let your whole body swoop and turn — so you can feel the motion. Have fun fluttering!

WHAT YOU NEED:

- 8¹/₂" x 11" (21 cm x 27.5 cm) tracing paper or white typing paper
- 8¹/₂" x 11" (21 cm x 27.5 cm) white construction paper or tag board
- Glue or tape
- Popsicle sticks
- Scissors
- Crayons or markers

WHAT YOU DO:

1. Trace the butterfly stencil from page 76 onto a piece of tracing paper.
2. Cut the tracing out and glue it onto the white construction paper or tag board.
3. Color the butterfly with crayons or markers. Add the two scent gland spots on wings to make a male butterfly, if you like. (For a review of how to tell the male and female apart, see page 33.)
4. Cut the butterfly out and glue it to a Popsicle stick, leaving enough stick showing to use as a handle.
5. Now, lift your butterfly puppet up and down, so you feel the air pushing under its wings. Flutter-by, butterfly!

Popsicle stick

Monarch Magic T-Shirt

Here's a fun T-shirt to wear. Make several and sell them at a "Save the Monarch" fund-raiser (see page 64). Put the caterpillar on the front and the butterfly on the back; then, add a phrase to your drawing such as "Save the Monarch" or "Think Milkweed." Your T-shirt will send an important message to everyone you meet!

WHAT YOU NEED:

- Caterpillar stencil (see page 78)
- Butterfly stencil (see page 79)
- 50% cotton/50% polyester T-shirt
- Fabric crayons
- White paper, 6 sheets
- Grown-up helper
- Iron (for grown-up use only)

WHAT YOU DO:

1. Trace the caterpillar and butterfly onto separate sheets of white paper. Color with the fabric crayons, pressing hard so the colors are dark.
2. Place several sheets of white paper between the front and back of your shirt. Then, lay the caterpillar design colored-side down on your T-shirt front and cover with white paper.
3. Ask a grown-up to iron the stencil (cotton setting; no steam) to your T-shirt for at least 2 minutes, or until you can see the image coming off the paper.

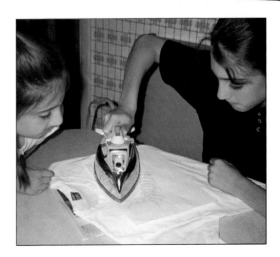

4. Carefully lift one corner of the stencil and peek at the colors. Continue ironing to make darker if necessary. Remove the paper image and let it cool.
5. Repeat with the butterfly image on the T-shirt back.
6. Wear your monarch T-shirt with pride!

Washing Tip: Machine-wash your butterfly T-shirt in warm water on a gentle cycle. Line dry. Don't place in a dryer.

Lick-and-Stick Butterfly Stickers

Homemade stickers are great for sealing envelopes, decorating stationery, or sticking on notebooks. Just moisten the back and you're ready to start sticking!

WHAT YOU NEED:

- Paper, or pictures from magazines of monarch caterpillars and butterflies
- Scissors
- Markers or tempera paint
- 1 tablespoon (15 ml) flavored gelatin mix
- 2 tablespoons (25 ml) boiling water (grown-ups only!)
- Heatproof container
- Paintbrush

WHAT YOU DO:

1. Cut paper into butterfly or caterpillar shapes; then, draw or paint details colorfully.
2. To make "sticker gum," pour gelatin into a heatproof container. Ask a grown-up to add the boiling water. Stir until the gelatin is dissolved. Cool, but don't let harden.
3. Brush sticker gum onto the back of the shapes. Let the gum dry. Re-wet later when ready to use.
4. Stick on your butterfly stickers!

Crafty Tip: If the gelatin hardens, simply set the container in a pan of hot water to turn back to a liquid.

Butterfly Banquets

The monarchs' miraculous life cycle and magical migration give people so much joy. It's time to give the monarchs something back! Play host to butterflies in your backyard or in your window boxes by treating them to a sweet fruit feast and planting a butterfly garden. Help preserve the monarch caterpillars' only food source by creating milkweed wildspot gardens and collecting milkweed pods for a monarch retreat and caterpillar nursery. The projects here will help you thank the monarchs ... and help to preserve their milkweed habitat forever.

Diner's Delight

Serve the butterflies in your neighborhood a buffet of sweetened fruit. But don't expect only monarchs to show up; you're sure to get all sorts of insect visitors at your butterfly cafe!

WHAT YOU NEED:

- Ripe bananas
- Strawberries
- Watermelon
- Apples
- Sugar water
- Honey

WHAT YOU DO:

1. Slice the fruit into a flat bowl, plastic container, or pie tin. (Make enough for the butterflies — and some for you, too!)
2. Make sugar water by mixing 2 to 3 teaspoonfuls (10 to 15 ml) of sugar and honey into about 1/2 cup (125 ml) water.

Add the sweetened water to the fruit.
3. Place the dish on a porch, a bench, or in the garden. (Don't sit close to your concoction, however. Bees like this snack, too!)
4. Watch as the butterflies (and other flying friends) arrive for dinner!

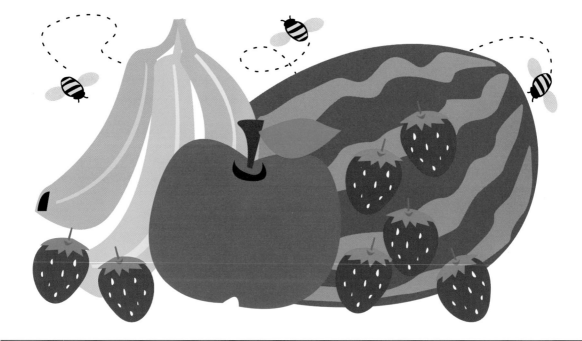

Another Hang-Up

Have a grown-up heat a nail in a candle. Then, poke two holes on opposite sides of a plastic container (the hot nail will melt the plastic). Thread string through the holes and tie the ends. Fill the container and hang it for the butterflies!

Caution! Hot!

Plant a Butterfly Garden!

Attract butterflies to your yard by planting a butterfly-friendly oasis! Soaring and gliding above mountains and hills, butterflies on the move need to stop for rest and nourishment. Each butterfly uses its long strawlike *proboscis*, or foldable tongue, to eagerly sip nectar from wildflowers along roadsides, in fields, and in meadows. You can help the butterflies out by growing flowers they like and planting them in such a way that the butterflies will be sure to find them. Even a simple patio garden or window box can be a stopover for a traveling monarch!

WHAT YOU NEED:

- Monarch journal (see page 46)
- Flower seeds or plants (see lists)
- A grown-up helper
- Garden shovel and rake
- Watering can

WHAT YOU DO:

Seek out the sun. The first thing to look for in choosing a butterfly garden site is lots of sun. Though butterflies can feed in the shade, they need sun to keep their bodies warm and their wings ready for flight. In your monarch journal, draw a map of your yard and record which areas get the most sun from 10:00 a.m. to 2:00 p.m. Or, look out your windows to see which window gets the most sun for a window-box garden. Once you've picked the perfect spot, ask a grown-up for permission (and help) to prepare the soil.

Plan the menu. Some flowers, because of their shape and the amount of nectar they hold, are easier for a butterfly to sip from than others. Pages 84 and 85 list some butterfly favorites that do well in full sun and with moderate watering. You can buy seeds and plants from garden centers or nurseries, supermarkets, or order through the mail.

Milkweed
(Asclepias)

Place milkweed plants in the center of your garden. They are what the butterflies like best! Their beautiful fragrance, sweet nectar, and pretty blossoms will attract not only monarchs, but many other butterflies and insects of all shapes, sizes, and colors.

Common milkweed (*Asclepias syriaca*) is the most widespread milkweed in the eastern U.S. It grows 3' to 5' (1 to 1.5 m) tall. Perennial. (See page 88 for tips on transplanting.)

Showy milkweed (*Asclepias speciosa*) is native to most of the western U. S. It has fragrant star-shaped pink and white flowers and round seed pods. It grows 3' to 4' (1 m) tall. Perennial.

Bloodflower (*Asclepias curassavica,* also called tropical milkweed or Mexican milkweed) is one of the best milkweeds to use in gardens and greenhouses because the seeds are simple to germinate and can be easily transplanted. It can be grown as an annual flower (planting it every year) in areas with frost. It has beautiful red and yellow flowers and slender seed pods, and grows 2' to 3' (1 m) tall. Tropical perennial.

Common Milkweed

Window Gardens

Looking for something that fits in a window? Cosmos, marigolds, and zinnias are all about the same height, and they're easy to grow from seed. Just fill the container about halfway up with growing mix (available from hardware stores or nurseries), moisten it with water, and start planting!

Butterflyweed *(Asclepias tuberosa)*. The bright orange flower heads attract monarchs and many other butterflies. The plants are easy to grow and need little care. Start with plants from a nursery or grow your own from seed. Grows 1' to 2' (1 m) tall; blooms midsummer on. Perennial.

Swamp milkweed *(Asclepias incarnata)* grows 2' to 4' (1 m) tall and is found in most of the eastern and central U.S. Seeds must be started outdoors in the fall or chilled before spring planting (see page 90). Or purchase as plants from a nursery. Perennial.

Bloodflower

Butterfly bush
(Buddleia davidii)
This shrub grows 3' to 6' (1 to 2 m) tall and comes in shades of purple, pink, and white. You can buy it in a pot from a nursery and transplant it to your garden.

Lantana
(Lantana camara)
This tender perennial won't make it through the winter where temperatures dip below 10°F (-12°C), but no matter where you live, you can buy these plants in spring and grow them for one summer.

Other Good Butterfly Bets

coreopsis *(Coreopsis lanceolata)*: Perennial. Grows 2'-3' (1 m).

cosmos *(Cosmos bipinnatus)*: Annual. Comes in a wide variety of colors. Easy to grow. Reseeds itself.

hollyhocks *(Alcea rosea)*: Perennial. Spiral blossoms grow on 4' to 6' (1 to 2 m) flower spikes.

lavender *(Lavandula)*: Perennial. Sweet-smelling herb garden plant.

liatris *(Liatris spicata)*: Perennial. This fuzzy purple flower is a favorite of monarchs! Flowers bloom into fall.

marigolds *(Tagetes)*: Annual. Favorite for beds and borders in gardens.

phlox *(Phlox)*: Annual and perennial. Showy summer pastel flowers.

purple coneflower *(Echinacea purpurea)*: Perennial. Showy daisy-like flowers grow 3' to 4' (1 m) tall.

zinnias *(Zinnia)*: Annual. Known for its brilliant show of colors when planted in masses.

A *perennial* flower regrows and reflowers year after year without replanting. Its roots can make it through the winter cold. *Annuals* die in the fall and must be replanted every year.

Seeds by Mail (and on the Web)

Many mail-order companies sell flower mixes for butterfly gardens, as well as specific seeds and plants. Try your local nursery or garden center, or write to one of these companies:

W. Atlee Burpee & Co.
300 Park Ave., Warminster, PA 18974; phone (800) 333-5888; Web site http://www.garden@burpee.com

Shepherd's Garden Seeds
30 Irene St., Torrington, CT 06790; phone (860) 482-3638

Vermont Wildflower Farm
P.O. Box 5, Route 7, Charlotte, VT 05445-0005; phone (802) 425-3500 or 1-800-424-1165

White Flower Farm
P.O. Box 50
Litchfield, CT 06759-9988 (plants)

For milkweed seeds and a guide to the best choices for your area, contact:

Butterfly Encounters
http://www.butterflyfarm.com

The Butterfly Website
http://www.mgfx.com/butterfly/

Ready, set,

Starting outdoors.

1. In the spring, after the threat of frost is past, prepare the soil in your chosen garden spot by breaking up the clods of dirt.
2. Drag two fingers pressed together through the soil — about 1" (2.5 cm) deep — in a row, in a circle, or in a design.
3. Water the rows, drop in the seeds (they are tiny, but try to spread them out), and cover with a sprinkling of loose soil. Pat soil firmly.
4. Keep seeds well watered but not soaked.
5. Once the seedlings poke through the soil, "thin" them by pulling some up. They should be 10" to 12" (25 to 30 cm) apart to grow well.

plant!

Starting outdoors.

1. Early in the spring, fill some small peat pots, egg cartons, or milk cartons with potting soil.
2. Plant seeds in containers; then, place them in the sunniest window of your home.
3. Keep the soil moist. In a week or two your seeds will sprout, or germinate.
4. Once the ground begins to warm up (and frost warnings are past), transplant the seedlings to your growing site.

Buying seedlings: If you buy small plants from a nursery, dig holes for them, fill the holes with water, and then plant. Water, wait, and watch for blooms — and butterflies!

Make a butterfly garden scrapbook with photos, your art, graphs, and journal entries of what happened on certain dates. Here are some ideas to get you started:

• Count all the visiting butterflies and insects; get a book to help you identify them by name; make a chart or graph of how many you see each day. Record your observations (with the date) in your monarch journal.

• Take photos of flowers and butterflies in different stages of growth and glue them in your monarch journal (with a date).

• Paint a watercolor picture.

Warning!
Pesticides and herbicides can be fatal to butterflies. Never use them in your garden!

A Butterfly Puddle

Add a watering hole to give the butterflies a place to drink. Fill a shallow basin with sand, soil, and pebbles, and enough water to make it puddly but not so wet that the butterflies will get soaked.

Grow a Wildspot Milkweed Garden!

It's time for action! Kids across North and Central America — from Canada all the way to Mexico — can be the leaders in saving the monarchs' milkweed habitats, and help save the monarch itself!

How can you make such a big difference? If every kid — whether in city, suburb, or rural area — would grow several milkweed plants each year in safe places near homes and schools, the monarchs' milkweed habitats would continue to thrive. It's as simple as that.

WHAT YOU NEED:

- A sunny garden spot or patio container
- Shovel
- Milkweed plants
- Watering can

WHAT YOU DO:

1. In the spring or early summer, prepare a planting site in a sunny spot at the edge of your lawn or in a patio planter. You don't need a big area. Use a shovel to dig a hole that's 1 to 2 feet (30 to 60 cm) deep in the ground where you want to plant, or fill a 1- to 2-foot-wide (30 to 60 cm) planter halfway with soil.

2. With a grown-up, look for young, green milkweed plants growing in a vacant lot, along roadsides, or in a field that will soon be mowed. Use the shovel to dig a large circle around the stem, being careful not to injure the roots.

Let's Do It!

For even more fun, try collecting milkweed seeds in the fall and planting a milkweed wildspot garden from seed (see page 90). Add some nectar plants for a colorful butterfly retreat (page 83).

3. Lift up the root ball and carry it to your new planting site.

4. Add a gallon of water to your prepared hole; then, place your milkweed plant into the hole or container. Fill in around the plant with soil. Press the soil down firmly.

5. Water your plant every other day. As you watch the milkweed grow, keep an eye out for the first monarchs to arrive!

Collect (and Grow) Your Own Milkweed Seeds!

The silky white seed puffs that burst from the milkweed pod in autumn are more than a wonderful show: They are the source of next spring's milkweed plants! By collecting the seeds in fall, after the first frost, as the pods pop open, you'll be able to grow your own milkweed plants from seed, and have plenty of seed to share with friends and neighbors (see page 62). Experiment with fall or spring planting — or both — to see which works best where you live. Get your friends involved, too!

WHAT YOU NEED:

- A small plastic container with a lid (such as a cottage cheese container)
- Plastic sandwich bags
- Shovel
- Milk containers and peat-based growing mix (for spring planting only)

WHAT YOU DO:

Collect milkweed seeds in the fall after the first frost, when the milkweed pods pop open. Act fast: The seed puffs will float away in the wind! Gather up the pods, remove the white puffs, and place them in the plastic container. Indoors (where it's not windy), separate out the brown seeds, and save them in a plastic sandwich bag. Toss away the white fluff.

Gardener's Tip:

Milkweed seeds have tough outer skins that sometimes make it difficult for the little plant inside to get started. If your seeds don't sprout, ask a grown-up to carefully cut the smooth, straight edge off each seed with a razor blade. This gives the plant an opening to grow through. In warm areas where there's no frost over the winter, you may need to refrigerate your seeds for several months before planting them in the fall or spring.

Fall planting:

1. Prepare the soil in a sunny wildspot garden site by turning it over with a shovel.
2. Scatter the seeds on the newly turned soil, and sprinkle them with soil.
3. Next spring, look for your new milkweed plants!

Spring planting:

1. Store seeds collected in fall in a cold, dark place (the crisper in your refrigerator works well) for at least two months.
2. In early spring, plant the prechilled seeds indoors in moistened peat pots or milk cartons filled with damp peat-based seed-starting mix. Plant the seeds about $1/8$" (3 mm) deep and cover them with a sprinkle of soil. Keep the soil moist (but not soggy) and place the pots in a sunny, warm window.
3. Transplant your seedlings into your wildspot garden when the weather is warm and frost warnings are past. Watch them grow, and wait for the butterflies to find them!

Seeds ¢

Butterfly Milkweed
Asclepias tuberosa

Seeds ¢

White Milkweed
Asclepias variegata

No Milkweed?

Can't find any milkweed plants to transplant or collect seed from? No problem. Check your local nursery or gardening center for milkweed plants, or order seeds by mail (see pages 84 and 86 for seed sources and the names of specific types of milkweed that will grow in your area). You'll be introducing a wonderful plant to your neighborhood!

Index

More Books from Williamson Publishing

Williamson books are available from your bookseller or directly from Williamson Publishing. Please see last page for ordering information or to visit our website.

Other *Good Times!* Books

KIDS' PUMPKIN PROJECTS
Planting & Harvest Fun
by Deanna F. Cook
Ages 4-10. 96 pages, fully illustrated, trade paper,
8 x 10, $8.95 US.

Kids Can!® Books

The following *Kids Can!®* books for ages 4 to 10 are each 160-178 pages, fully illustrated, trade paper, 11 x 8 1/2, $12.95 US.

American Bookseller Pick of the Lists
Oppenheim Toy Portfolio Gold Seal Award
Benjamin Franklin Juvenile Nonfiction Book of the Year
Learning Magazine® Teachers' Choice Award
SUPER SCIENCE CONCOCTIONS
50 Mysterious Mixtures for Fabulous Fun
by Jill Frankel Hauser

GIZMOS & GADGETS
Creating Science Contraptions that Work
  (& Knowing Why)
by Jill Frankel Hauser

Benjamin Franklin Science and Education Award
Oppenheim Toy Portfolio Gold Seal Award
American Bookseller Pick of the Lists
THE KIDS' SCIENCE BOOK
Creative Experiences for Hands-On Fun
by Robert Hirschfeld and Nancy White

Dr. Toy Best Vacation Product Award
CUT-PAPER PLAY!
Dazzling Creations from Construction Paper
by Sandi Henry

Early Childhood News Directors' Choice Award
VROOM! VROOM!
Making 'dozers, 'copters, trucks & more
by Judy Press

BOREDOM BUSTERS!
The Curious Kids' Activity Book
by Avery Hart & Paul Mantell

MAKING COOL CRAFTS & AWESOME ART!
A Kids' Treasure Trove of Fabulous Fun
by Roberta Gould

Dr. Toy Best Vacation Product Winner
THE KIDS' NATURE BOOK
365 Indoor/Outdoor Activities & Experiences
by Susan Milord

Benjamin Franklin Best Multicultural Book Award
Parents' Choice Approved!
Skipping Stones Multicultural Honor Award
THE KIDS' MULTICULTURAL COOKBOOK
Food & Fun Around the World
by Deanna F. Cook

KIDS' COMPUTER CREATIONS
Using Your Computer for Art & Craft Fun
by Carol Sabbeth

Parents' Choice Approved!
Dr. Toy Best Vacation Product Award
KIDS GARDEN!
The Anytime, Anyplace Guide to Sowing &
  Growing Fun
by Avery Hart and Paul Mantell

Parents' Choice Gold Award
American Bookseller Pick of the Lists
Oppenheim Toy Portfolio Best Book
THE KIDS' MULTICULTURAL ART BOOK
Art & Craft Experiences from Around the World
by Alexandra M. Terzian

Parents' Choice Gold Award!
Benjamin Franklin Best Juvenile Nonfiction Award

KIDS MAKE MUSIC!
Clapping and Tapping from Bach to Rock
by Avery Hart and Paul Mantell

American Bookseller Pick of the Lists
Dr. Toy Best Vacation Product Award

KIDS' CRAZY CONCOCTIONS
50 Mysterious Mixtures for Art & Craft Fun
by Jill Frankel Hauser

American Bookseller Pick of the Lists
Oppenheim Toy Portfolio Gold Seal Award
Skipping Stones Nature & Ecology Honor Award

EcoArt!
Earth-Friendly Art & Craft Experiences for
  3- to 9-Year-Olds
by Laurie Carlson

Selection of Newbridge / Better Homes & Gardens / Scholastic
book clubs

KIDS COOK!
Fabulous Food for the Whole Family
by Sarah Williamson and Zachary Williamson

THE KIDS' WILDLIFE BOOK
Exploring Animal Worlds through Indoor/Outdoor
  Crafts & Experiences
by Warner Shedd

HANDS AROUND THE WORLD
365 Creative Ways to Build Cultural Awareness &
  Global Respect
by Susan Milord

KIDS CREATE!
Art & Craft Experiences for 3- to 9-Year-Olds
by Laurie Carlson

Parents Magazine Parents' Pick!

KIDS LEARN AMERICA!
Bringing Geography to Life with People, Places &
  History
by Patricia Gordon and Reed C. Snow

American Bookseller Pick of the Lists

ADVENTURES IN ART
Art & Craft Experiences for 8- to 13-Year-Olds
by Susan Milord

Benjamin Franklin Science and Education Award

HAND-PRINT ANIMAL ART
by Carolyn Carreiro
full color, $14.95

Kaleidoscope Kids™ Books —Where Learning Meets Life

***Kaleidoscope Kids*™ books allow children, ages 6 to 10, to explore a subject from many different angles, using many different skills. All books are 96 pages, 2-color, fully illustrated, 10 x 10, $10.95 US.**

Children's Book Council Notable Book
American Bookseller Pick of the Lists
Dr. Toy 10 Best Educational Products

PYRAMIDS!
50 Hands-On Activities to Experience Ancient Egypt
by Avery Hart & Paul Mantell

KNIGHTS & CASTLES
50 Hands-On Activities to Experience the Middle Ages
by Avery Hart & Paul Mantell

ANCIENT GREECE!
50 Hands-On Activities to Experience This
  Wondrous Age
by Avery Hart and Paul Mantell

MEXICO!
50 Activities to Experience Mexico Past & Present
by Susan Milord

Little Hands® Books

The following *Kids Can!*® books for ages 2 to 6 are each 144 pages, fully illustrated, trade paper, 10 x 8, $12.95 US.

SCIENCE PLAY
Beginning Discoveries for 2- to 6-Year-Olds
by Jill Frankel Hauser

American Bookseller Pick of the Lists

RAINY DAY PLAY!
Explore, Create, Discover, Pretend
by Nancy Fusco Castaldo

Parents' Choice Gold Award
Children's Book-of-the-Month Club Selection

FUN WITH MY 5 SENSES
Activities to Build Learning Readiness
by Sarah A. Williamson